OPTIMISING EDUCATIONAL ENVIRONMENT THROUGH CREATIVITY

DR DHEERAJ MEHROTRA

Copyright © Dr Dheeraj Mehrotra
All Rights Reserved.

This book has been self-published with all reasonable efforts taken to make the material error-free by the author. No part of this book shall be used, reproduced in any manner whatsoever without written permission from the author, except in the case of brief quotations embodied in critical articles and reviews.

The Author of this book is solely responsible and liable for its content including but not limited to the views, representations, descriptions, statements, information, opinions and references ["Content"]. The Content of this book shall not constitute or be construed or deemed to reflect the opinion or expression of the Publisher or Editor. Neither the Publisher nor Editor endorse or approve the Content of this book or guarantee the reliability, accuracy or completeness of the Content published herein and do not make any representations or warranties of any kind, express or implied, including but not limited to the implied warranties of merchantability, fitness for a particular purpose. The Publisher and Editor shall not be liable whatsoever for any errors, omissions, whether such errors or omissions result from negligence, accident, or any other cause or claims for loss or damages of any kind, including without limitation, indirect or consequential loss or damage arising out of use, inability to use, or about the reliability, accuracy or sufficiency of the information contained in this book.

Made with ♥ on the Notion Press Platform
www.notionpress.com

Contents

Preface

Optimising Educational Environment Through Creativity, which targets learning, intercepts Grade-Level, Engaging, Affirming, and Meaningful. A topic dealt with priority enhances learning by doing and engaging.

Students are given the recognition within classrooms so that they may more easily follow the directions to concentrate their efforts. When a topic is given a higher priority for discussion, the opportunities for active participation in the discourse and direct experience in the subject matter increase. When a case is given a lower priority for discussion, the chances for both are reduced. The book deals with an understanding of the engaged learning module.

Happy Learning.

Author

www.authordheerajmehrota.com

1

Understanding GLEAM

Hey Friends,

I pondered the excellence model of learning and teaching and came across the term GLEAM, which absorbed my interest to know more. On learning more about the concept, it was when students participated in GLEAM teaching, and they were expected to build genuine links with their instructors. This is similar to what Zaretta Hammond suggests when she speaks about "learning partnerships," which is that students and teachers should work together to achieve a common goal.

GLEAM is an abbreviation for "global learning, engineering, arts, and mathematics." The explanation provided by Hammond is that to have effective learning partnerships, the teacher has to "build trust with students across differences so that they may create a social-emotional connection for deeper learning." The instructor must build a social-emotional connection with the kids to learn effectively.

The production of engaging lessons is based on the student's interests but not in the "edutainment" sense that the word is often understood to have. Students will have a greater chance of keeping their views about who they are, where they came from, and what they can become in the future if they are allowed to learn about topics of personal interest to them. Instructors who are aware of and responsible for the expectations that are placed on them by the curriculum in terms of the level of difficulty and the amount of constructive effort that should be expected from them are the ones who are responsible for delivering instruction that engages students. These instructors utilize their students' academic, linguistic, local-contextual, and cultural identities as on-ramps to the learning process in such a manner that increases their students' "intellectual capacity" (Hammond, 2015).

Affirming teaching is when students' ethnic, racial, and linguistic identities, as well as their recent and past experiences, are acknowledged and honoured within the framework of the assignments they are expected to complete at their grade level. This acknowledgement and honouring occur within the terms students are expected to complete at their grade level. These identities are incorporated into the framework of the tasks they are required to accomplish at the grade level they are currently enrolled in. Teachers committed to providing their students with an affirming education will explain or demonstrate how students may apply what they have learned to their own lives and the wider world. These educators recognize, value, and validate all aspects of their students' identities, including the intellectual and interpersonal facets of their student's lives and their entire humanity. This is accomplished by recognizing, valuing, and acknowledging all aspects of their student's lives.

Students are allowed to acquire information, reflect on the world, and then determine (with critique) how that knowledge may progress both the learner and the world. This process is called the information acquisition cycle. These changes may be accessed via teaching that is pertinent to the topic at hand. Teachers who can provide students with meaningful education do things like make room in the curriculum for students to develop their socio-political lenses by participating in activities such as conversation, discussion, questioning, writing, and thinking.

Other things that teachers who can provide students with a meaningful education do include the following: The following are some further examples of activities that fall within this category: To equip their students with a more comprehensive educational experience, these educators cultivate their own in-depth subject matter expertise and construct a cultural lens that is based on the children's perspective on the surrounding environment.

https://www.unbounded.org/blog/what-is-gleam reports the facts about GLEAM.

It is possible to disassemble the acronym GLEAM into its constituent pieces: grade-level appropriateness, engagement, affirmation, and meaning.

The phrase "grade-level appropriateness, engagement, affirmation, and meaning" uses the GLEAM abbreviation. These are the elements that go into constructing the acronym as a whole. The acronym comprises these four distinct parts, which, when placed together, *form the whole phrase. It is common practice to refer to this assertion using its acronym, GLEAM. The original version of this sentence was written out in its entirety. The statement is presented here in its most comprehensive understanding, represented by the acronym. The pupils have been given this abbreviation to make it easier to follow the guidelines supplied to them to concentrate their efforts. When a subject is given a higher priority for discussion, there is a more significant likelihood of individuals having direct experience with the issue and taking an active role in the conversation surrounding it. This is since the relevance of the case has recently increased. This is because, at the level at which a subject is scheduled to be discussed, that subject will always be accorded a greater priority for discussion. This may be attributed to the fact that a topic is always given higher importance for being discussed. When a problem is given a lesser priority for attention, there are fewer feasible topics to address, resulting in fewer opportunities for discussion and argument. This is because there are not as many themes to choose from.*

It is possible to recognize instructors with attitudes that support the GLEAM framework based on their characteristics. Some of these characteristics are discussed in more detail below.

Intellectual requirements for the grade level they teach, and they are open to expanding their understanding of the various cultures and conditions in which their students find themselves.

Consider the possibility that students will be able to satisfy the grade level requirements if they demonstrate their knowledge in various ways, using information pertinent to the topic at hand and several different approaches. In this scenario, the criteria for the grade level will have been fulfilled. Take into consideration this other possibility. In this scenario, the first step in developing a sense of agency in the fight against racism is understanding the role that racism plays in the educational systems utilized from kindergarten through high school. This understanding can be obtained by learning about the role that racism plays in the educational methods used. This comprehension may be accomplished by gaining a knowledge of the part that racism plays in the educational systems that are currently in use. This is the circumstance we find ourselves in due to the need to carry out the first step, which involves understanding the role that racism plays in these educational institutions. Because of this, you will have a more in-depth comprehension of the several methods in which you may fight bias.

Students are more likely to meet education and classroom experiences that are engaging, relevant, and affirming when GLEAM teaching is implemented. In addition, the expectations put on them at the appropriate grade level are met by the activities they participate in. This can be done since the skills, information, and attitudes represented by GLEAM education are helpful for kids of any academic background and transferable to those youngsters.

The following frames of mind are kept in mind by teachers when they are organizing lessons, and one of the ways that they can do this is by participating in activities such as those listed below:

Students must show a solid devotion to learning about the cultural resources to which they have access, in addition to their intellectual and personal identities. When addressing themes such as global literature, the significance of this point becomes very clear.

Continue to think about the individual identities and cultures that students bring into the classroom and the impact that these identities and cultures have on the relationships between students and the teaching they receive. In addition, think about the impact these identities and cultures have on the relationships between students outside of the classroom. In addition, give some thought to the influence these kids' varying cultures and identities have on the connections they develop with one another outside of the classroom. Additionally, give some attention to the impact these children's various cultures and uniqueness have on their bonds with one another outside of the school. This is something that should be taken into consideration. In addition, pay some attention to the influence that the children's diverse cultures and identities have on their relationships with one another outside of the classroom setting. These children come from various backgrounds and have a lot in common with one another. This is something that has to be taken into account, so keep that in mind.

Always be on the lookout for new facts about

curricula, pedagogy, and the many forms that racism may take both within and outside K-12 educational institutions. This pertains to the educational institutions providing kindergarten through 12th-grade instruction and the larger society. This is true for the K-12 educational systems as well as for the K-12 educational systems by themselves and by themselves alone. This holds not just for the K-12 educational systems as a whole but also the K-12 ones were taken on their own and their own exclusively.

These mentalities and planning practices are required for GLEAM instruction to occur; the people that educators are on a personal level and the activities they engage in outside of the classroom significantly impact how they instruct. GLEAM instruction is a multidisciplinary approach to education that focuses on the development of 21st-century skills. Instruction in GLEAM is an interdisciplinary approach to education that emphasizes developing skills appropriate for the 21st century. The pedagogical approach known as GLEAM is built on the idea that students learn best when actively engaged in the activity being taught to them. This is the central tenet of the GLEAM methodology.

GLEAM has the potential to change long-standing inequities in our educational system, such as students' unequal access to learning at their appropriate grade level and the unfair distribution of opportunities for students to be seen, heard, and valued. These inequities have been present for a long time, and GLEAM has the potential to change these long-standing inequities. These injustices have existed for a significant amount of time, and there is a possibility that GLEAM will brings about a shift in these long-standing inequities. These long-standing disparities have persisted for a considerable length of time, and there is a chance that GLEAM will will change these unfair conditions' trajectory. These long-standing inequalities have lasted for a substantial amount of time, and there is a possibility that GLEAM may brings about a shift in the trajectory of these unjust circumstances. GLEAM is an acronym for "Global Education and Empowerment of Minorities and Women."

These long-standing inequities have persisted for a considerable length of time, and there is a chance that GLEAM may changes the path these unfair conditions are on. Global Education and Empowerment of Women and Minorities is what "GLEAM" stands for in its full name. This is a possibility that genuinely piques our attention. In upcoming blog postings, we will investigate the specifics of what GLEAM training consists of and the issues that are covered by it. To accomplish this, it will be necessary to take a more in-depth look at what happens in classrooms when the mindset of teachers and the planning they do together serve the purpose of providing engaging education that is affirming and meaningful and appropriate for the level of the class.

2

The Classroom Creativity

Improving one's ability to think critically

It is one of the most essential facets and abilities that students need to focus on, and it is also referred to as cognitive thinking. It is to prepare pupils for the worst-case scenario if one goes by the literal meaning of critical thinking, which is to grasp the objective examination and assessment of a problem to develop a decision. Students have a tendency to rack their brains on complex subjects to make it easier for themselves, which is why the role of critical thinking in 21st-century learning allows students to improve their academic understanding. In addition, having an understanding of the subject is helpful when conducting dialogues and discussions on a wide range of subjects. The ability to think critically is beneficial because it enables one to evaluate a situation or subject in a more rational manner and to come to a choice that is based on accurate information.

Teamwork, collaboration, and other forms of cooperation

Collaboration is of the utmost importance since the majority of the world's operations have shifted to taking place behind a screen and, as a result necessitate being linked with individuals from all over the globe. In point of fact, this fundamental ability of collaboration is and will continue to be the cornerstone of a successful student in the long term. Not only does the idea of working together in harmony and cooperation with other students assist kids in acquiring an awareness of the people around them, but it also teaches them how to negotiate their relationships with one another. This capacity to synchronize ultimately manifests itself in the job, socially, and at home with friends and family. The importance of respecting other people and their perspectives and being an influential member of a team working toward a common objective is emphasized. Overall, working with others and contributing to a group effort are two fundamental abilities that will serve students *well in the future workplace.*

Keep in mind that communication is the most important thing.

As educators, it is essential to have strong listening and open and honest communication skills; the two go hand in hand. One can only speak well without coming across as problematic if one can listen attentively since this is the only way to do so. Even when one disagrees with anything, it is essential to speak courteously and be a good listener. When you do so, you help develop a stronger connection and a healthier relationship that demonstrates respect for the people around you. Patience is created along with the practice of this skill. Both creative ability and imaginative capacity Creativity, in the same vein as critical thinking, is a good workout for the brain and is something that everyone has in plenty.

Creativity accomplishes the same goals as critical thinking but in a far more relaxed and enjoyable way than critical thinking does. To encourage kids to think creatively and develop original ideas, it is essential to stimulate their imaginations and provide them with the freedom to experiment with novel situations.

Participating in a variety of activities that allow individuals and groups to exhibit their creative potential is something that everyone should do. Aside from the competencies above, students in the 21st century will also need to be proficient in the following learning abilities: literacy in technology, adaptability, fundamental life skills, the ability to take the initiative, leadership, social responsibility, and cultural awareness.

3

Classroom Management Skills

1. Giving a lecture

It's possible to give a lecture in the style of educational discourse, but it may also be delivered as an authoritative monologue. Some of the challenges presented by lectures may be circumvented by encouraging interaction between the instructor and the students via the use of questions and responses. The class has to be Engaging, Informative, Creative, Thought-provoking, Comprehending, and Relevant while also being Fun to Take.

2. Activities During the Roundabout Time

Circle time, sometimes referred to as group time, is when a group of individuals sit together to participate in an activity that includes everyone. The purpose of circle time, which is often a lighthearted and enjoyable activity, is to make youngsters ready for learning. Take into consideration the following three fundamental questions: why what, and how.

3. The Method of Simulation

Bringing life into classrooms by use of The term "simulations" refers to many types of learning situations in which the student is immersed in a "world" created by the instructor. They are a representation of a world in which the pupils participate. This "Engagement" is governed by the boundaries that are set by the instructor, who also makes use of it to fulfil the educational goals that have been set.

4. Modelling Method

Modelling is a method of education in which the instructor shows a new idea or method of learning to the class, and the students learn via watching and mimicking their instructor's actions. When a teacher takes the time to explain a topic to a student, that teacher is modelling for the learner. It stimulates participation in an essential way.

5. Educational Resources to Be Found Online

The following is a list of the most widely used digital education tools for both educators and students. Edmodo is one of the most widespread examples; it is a platform that functions as both an educational instrument and a social network, connecting students and instructors. Google Classrooms and Kahoot are other systems that get a lot of usage.

6. A Simulation of a Game

The instructor places a high priority on meeting the specific requirements of each student when they make use of simulation games, which is one of the cutting-edge methods of education. During this process stage, learning should be seen as an active rather than a passive process. Students need to look closely at not just their values but also the values of others around them, in particular.

7. Approaches to Solving Problems Together

Highly collaborative problem-solving can be defined as "the capacity of an individual to effectively engage in a process whereby two or more agents attempt to solve a problem by sharing the understanding and effort required to come up with a solution and pooling their knowledge and skills in totality." This process involves two or more people attempting to solve a problem by sharing the understanding and effort required to come up with a solution. Learning is made more active via the use of hands-on activities.

8. Groups for Open Dialogue

The Discussion style of teaching is a group activity in which the instructor and the student work together to define the issue and determine how to solve it. It is a productive approach that emphasises listening, thinking, and developing conversational skills as a top priority.

9. Instruction from Peers

The concept that "to teach is to learn twice" is the foundation for peer teaching, which is one or more students instructing other students in a certain subject area. Peer teaching is built on "to teach is to learn twice" (Whitman, 1998).
" For students, learning from their peers may result in better attitudes as well as a learning experience that is more personalized, engaging, and collaborative, ultimately leading to greater levels of academic accomplishment. Peer instructors may find that the experience increases their comprehension of the material and boosts their confidence in their abilities.

10. Participatory Instruction

Active learning is a form of education that includes actively engaging students with the subject matter being taught in the classroom using a variety of approaches such as conversations, problem-solving, case studies, role plays, and other activities. The next step will include providing pupils with a time restriction to finish the activity. The plan calls for a halt to the activity and conducting a debriefing. Ask a few students or student groups to offer their perspectives, and then incorporate those ideas into the subsequent parts of your presentation.

11. Instruction Focused on Projects

Students learn knowledge and skills via Project-Based Learning, a teaching technique in which they work for a long period to study and answer a real-world topic, problem, or challenge that is genuine, engaging, and difficult. Teachers that use the project-based approach to education make it their priority to ensure that students comprehend the learning objectives and the significance of why they are important while they are still impressionable.

12. In-Unit Evaluations

To evaluate the efficacy of the school's overall teaching and learning process, students are given periodic examinations in the classroom. The primary objective of the unit test is to separate each component of the system from locating, investigating, and correcting any flaws that may be present. In the following way toward greatness, the exam is distinct from assessments and evaluations.

13. Duties and obligations

The approach known as "Assignments" is by far the most often used instructional strategy in schools today, especially regarding the instruction of Science. It is a method that is often implemented in the course of the teaching and learning process. It is a method of education that includes being directed through the content, learning on one's own, developing writing abilities, and preparing reports. In addition, some straightforward homework tasks are included as one of the most common forms of education and assessment.

14. Brain Gym and Quizzing in the Classroom:

Ask them questions to stimulate their brain and help them perform more effectively. Example: Have them use their thumbs together to create the number nine. Ask them to use their index finger to write their first name in English in the air.

15. Instruction in Corrective Matters

Locate struggling kids and encourage them to participate in peer instruction. Engage them by pairing them in activities, such as the 12:00 o'clock partner or other time intervals. Even before the morning assembly or in the afternoon, this can take place.

16. Displays and Presentations

Interact with them using your presenting abilities while using technology. PREZI, Microsoft Powerpoint, and KEYNOTE are only a few presenting tools that are extensively utilized.

17. Zoom In

Give the children the opportunity to look at progressively more significant parts of a picture, then encourage them to write and get involved in writing. Inquire with them about the new things they have noticed. In what ways does it cause a shift in their thinking? Repeat the process of revealing something and asking questions until the whole picture is seen.

18. Chalk Talk

You may get their attention by analyzing their

schoolwork using the Chalk Talk Strategy. A chalk-speak approach is an excellent tool for igniting the interest of reserved kids. It gets the students involved, encourages independent thought, and gives each student an equal voice in the discussion. At this point, the instructor instructs the pupils to analyze how they have been thinking. The pupils work together as a team to cycle through the various challenges. The results are made available to the general audience.

19. Work on Books and Perform the Step-Inside Routine

Students have the opportunity to respond to questions digitally via Step Inside, thanks to this feature. You allow them to go into the personalities of various people. It's almost like you're immersing yourself in a specific circumstance. Appropriate for English and History classes that focus on analyzing historical events from a certain angle. Example Speculating about or pondering the experience of serving in the military.

20. Posters and Readers

Display the posters and encourage the youngsters to read them and participate in the discussion. This is accomplished via sporadic encounters with the student's classmates and the instructors. It includes Visual Literacy, as I see, I wonder. The utilization of posters and the provision of a chance to read the material alone or by a lucky system are immensely beneficial.

21. Instruments for Independent Study

This is a real-life illustration of how utilizing several learning tools may be a helpful method. Google Digital Garage, LinkedIn Learning, Coursera, Khan Academy, edX, and Academic Earth are all examples of helpful online learning resources.

22. Contests and Events

This encompasses many forms, such as debates, interactions, recitations, writing, fashion shows, speech contests, and presentations of case studies.

23. Learning Through Objects (OBL)

Active learning may also take the form of object-based education. An instructional strategy known as "student-centred learning" places the student's participation in learning in the classroom high on its priority list. The students must first practice the skills being taught, such as identifying and describing the main topic or activity in a class and giving some coherent, sequenced details for it to be effective. The goal is to catch them when they are young and innocent toward learning as the ultimate goal.

25. Club Activities

This leads to improved body awareness, independent thinking, problem-solving and reasoning skills, positive self-image, talent management, cooperation, and collaboration. Co-curricular activities such as public speaking, debate and dramatics, creative writing, eco-club, quizzing, astronomy, dancing, photography, philately, hiking, film appreciation, and even cooking are some other activities which may be offered.

26. Adaptable Instruction

Adaptive teaching is an educational strategy that seeks to accomplish a shared instructional objective with learners with individual variances, such as past success, aptitude, or learning styles that vary. It helps provide personalised learning to provide learners with learning pathways that are efficient, effective, and personalized to their needs. Additionally, it makes it easier for instructors to engage each student. It is a strategy of altering the direction and speed of learning that is driven by data collected from students, enabling personalised learning delivery at scale and in its entirety.

27. Learning That Crosses Over

A complete knowledge of learning that crosses formal and informal learning environments is what is meant when people talk about crossover learning. The end goal of crossover learning is to improve teaching. It is one of the approaches used in the provision of personalized learning and has as its primary objective the provision of learning pathways that are engaging, efficient, and individualized.

28. Study of a Case

Learning may be included in the case study process by having students participate in discussions on specific scenarios that replicate real-world instances, such as "Distractions Within Classrooms." This strategy places the learner at the centre of the experience and emphasizes active participation from all participants, including brainstorming. Because of this, they are forced to acquire new abilities, expand their knowledge base, and cooperate in investigating the case.

29. Learning by Oneself

Utilizing the Educational Tools Provided by Google Earth. Students can connect what they learn in the classroom and what they encounter in their everyday lives, communities, and the more fantastic globe. This helps them visualise abstract ideas over a global canvas. The creative tools that Google Earth offers will enable you to work on your ideas.

30. Team Projects

The creation of a poster, a PowerPoint presentation, the design of a model, the result of a shoebox diorama, the use of a three-panel display board, the creation of a timeline, the outcome of a board game that incorporates critical elements, and the writing of a poem are all examples of possible projects.

31. Investigational Projects

Students must undertake research on their initiative with no predetermined conclusions as part of a research-based instructional model. This approach to instruction and education emphasizes the lecturers' and students' shared participation in developing new abilities. In light of this, instructors must consider their roles as educators and students.

32. Gesturing

This method of instruction incorporates the learner's movements, which enables the indexing of occasions when conceptual clarity is lacking. During this procedure stage, the instructors will use such motions to assess a student's thought process. The students arrive at original concepts during the activity by analyzing the hand movements performed during a session.

33. Films That Teach This is a Common Way

Instructional videos are a widespread method that incorporates the display of learning via videos. The pupils are led in a specific direction via electronic instructions and movies, and learning is shown at various points along the process.

34. Social Media The most effective use of social media in education provides students with the opportunity to get more knowledge that benefits them. Because of this, they are linked with online learning groups and other educational platforms. The pupils can voice their questions, concerns, and observations, streamlining the educational process. These technologies enable students and educational institutions to investigate various possibilities to enhance learning techniques.

35. Humor The use of humour in the classroom investigates the beginnings of teaching methods that have seen substantial development over time. It makes it possible to move away from the conventional education delivery method, which includes tactics like recitation and memorization. In contrast, the interactive techniques that include humour as a priority now for sure with the march of time and tide as a reality in practice for schools and instructors need to dwell as a pastime for the time being are part of the current way of doing things.

The beginning is geared toward the participatory nature of students within classrooms in order to connect and make learning a priority for both the teacher and the learner in momentum to share the cause of education, making the best for all. The inception is eyed and segmented towards the participatory nature of students within classrooms.

36. Panel Discussion

During this particular kind of instruction, the first steps of the process consist of listening and observing. In a Panel Discussion, a predetermined or invited set of students acts as the panel, while the other students in the class function as the audience for the discussion.

A leader for the panel is selected, and they are responsible for providing a summary of the topic before opening the floor to the public. After completing the process for clarity and cooperation, there will be a question and answer session.

37. Modelling

Modelling is an instructional strategy in which the instructor demonstrates a new concept or an approach to make learning a priority with the preface of teaching excellence and the WOW spectrum towards the taste and requirements of the learners. Modelling can be used to make learning a focus with the foreword of teaching excellence and the WOW spectrum towards the taste and needs of the learners. During this stage, the pupils take pleasure in learning via observation. The learning takes place via statements.

When a teacher illustrates a topic for a student, the teacher is acting as a measure by modeling the notion for the learner.

38. The Method of Discovery

The "Guided Discovery" format, which refers to a teaching and learning environment in which students actively participate in discovering knowledge by exploring options through working and exploring ideas, is required for use with the Discovery Learning Method. This format is also known as the "Discovery Learning Method." It is a constructivist theory based on the idea that students construct their understanding and knowledge of the world by experiencing things and reflecting on those experiences. Specifically, it is based on the idea that students make their understanding and knowledge of the world through experience. It is an approach to education founded on the constructivist theory of learning, and inquiry-based teaching methods support it.

39. The Method of Demonstration

The demonstration module includes showcasing, in general, using the help of visuals like flip charts, posters, PowerPoint, and several other tools that may be accessed online or offline.

Walking someone through the stages of creating something or doing an activity step by step is known as a demonstration. It is appropriate for use in scientific fields.

40. The Method of Role Playing

Students are given the opportunity to explore real-life scenarios through the use of a method called role-playing, which involves students interacting with one another in a structured manner for the purpose of developing real-life skills and experiencing an environment that includes elements of choice and chance.

With the format of Role Playing, the kids get to experience an extra learning pleasure as a result, and they are better able to comprehend the situation that is being presented during the procedure.

41. Oral Questions

Thanks to this practice, the instructor can engage the pupils verbally via assignments. When questioning is done among the students, it begins and includes the instructor's participation.

The questions are posed to the participants so that they would reflect on what they already know about the subject at hand, and the responses are given verbally. The questions, in most cases, make it possible for the instructor to maintain the point of the conversation centered on the intended purpose and the learning target via the engagement of all students for an extended period.

42. The Method of Questioning

Questioning is a technique to ask Oral Questions, and it could also incorporate written tasks. The goal is to engage the students in meaningful work via the use of contacts and employment opportunities.

43. Discussion Method

Here, we will follow the collaborative exchange of ideas among the students to stimulate the student's thinking, learning, problem-solving, comprehension, and decision-making skills.

44. Instruction Centered Around Problems

This determines if the children are engaged in the learning process by using Question or Assignment based activities. The issue or assignment is given to the instructor, who then collaborates with the pupils and other relevant participants. During the review modules, this is one of the straightforward methods that may be used to test the students' knowledge.

45. Tasks and Duties

This includes tasks assigned at employment, regular jobs, assessments given in class, homework assignments, and online reflections.

46. Make sure that kids and instructors have access to open source and free technology.

The goal is to achieve certain links by following the guidelines of UNESCO. It is imperative that open educational materials and digital platforms with open access be promoted. Ready-made material developed outside of the pedagogical arena and apart from the human interactions that exist between instructors and students cannot foster healthy growth in educational institutions.

47. Learning That Crosses Over

The term "crossover learning format" refers, in its entirety, to an all-encompassing comprehension of learning that crosses the gap between the formal and casual learning environments seen in a classroom. Via this medium, education may be enriched with experiences from day-to-day life; informal understanding can be developed by adding questions and information gained at school.

This structure aims to give students the most beneficial aspects of formal and casual learning settings by combining the best elements of each. According to boardteachers.com, an efficient technique for implementing crossover learning is for educators to pose a question or problem to their students in the classroom, with the expectation that they will resolve the issue while on educational excursions to museums or other locations. Children might expand their knowledge by compiling a collection of photographs, making notes or asking others for their perspectives. They then bring what they've learnt back to the classroom to shed more excellent light on the issue presented to them.

48. Technique Dramatique

It is more comparable to the use of drama in the classroom or dramatics in educational settings. Students are then allowed to investigate various aspects of the curriculum utilizing a variety of Gardner's multiple intelligences. In this setting, the children are actively engaged in the educational process via the use of theatre as a practice. They are completely submerged in the topic through participating in the activities, and they act out different roles related to the issue of education in role plays. The procedure stimulates, over time, the development of their abilities and, in particular, their bodies, brains, and emotions, which ultimately increases the frequency with which they engage in creative and innovative activities.

49. Pen Pals

A term created in bygone years has taken on a new meaning in modern times. Through PenPal platforms, educators from around the globe discuss their experiences with global project-based learning. According to the statement made by one of the educational institutions that are putting this into practice, "We set the students up with their email accounts and placed them under one central email alias." The instructors may check each email conversation to ensure it is proper and then construct spelling lists and subject word banks based on the sales.

This was made possible as a result of the previous step. Because messages were now coming within seconds of the send button being pressed, we switched to having weekly talks, and we also switched to having weekly bargains. Our students could sail over the typical "getting to know you" inquiries and move on to subjects that allowed for real cultural connections due to this strategy.

50. Audio Tutorial Lessons

The format is also known as PODCASTING in a unique meaning, and it is used often in educational institutions. Audio tutorial instruction is the technique of aural presentation that instructors consider to be the most comprehensive and well-documented in practice among kids.

51. Mobile Applications

The use of mobile applications provides a significant contribution to the methodical learning process. The most exciting aspect of mobile learning, also known as m-learning, is that it consists of education delivered through the Internet with the assistance of various personal mobile devices. This is covered by the "Bring Your Own Device" (BYOD) format in schools, where students are encouraged to use their own tablets and smartphones to enhance their educational experience. It makes it easier to acquire learning resources by using social connections, mobile applications, and online educational hubs.

Dheeraj Mehrotra, MS, MPhil, PhD (Education Management) honoris causa., a white and a yellow belt in SIX SIGMA, a Certified NLP Business Diploma holder, is an Educational Innovator, Author, with expertise in Six Sigma In Education, Academic Audits, Neuro-Linguistic Programming (NLP), Total Quality Management In Education, an Experiential Educator, a CBSE Resource towards School Assessment (SQAA), CCE, JIT, Five S, and KAIZEN. He has authored over 100 books on topics which include Computer Science, AI, Digital Body Language, NLP, Quality Circles, School Management, Classroom Effectiveness and Safety and security in schools.

A former Principal at De Indian Public School, New Delhi, (INDIA), NPS International School, Guwahati, and Education Officer at GEMS, Gurgaon, with an ample teaching experience of over Two Decades, he is a certified Trainer for Quality Circles/ TQM in Education and QCI Standards for School Accreditation/ School Audits and Management. He has also been honoured with the President of India's National Teacher Award in the year 2006 and the Best Science Teacher State Award (By the Ministry of Science and Technology, State of UP),

Innovation in Education for his inception of Six Sigma In Education by Education Watch, New Delhi and Education World- Best Teacher Award, BOLT Learner Teacher Award by Air India, 'Innovation in Education Award 2016' by Higher Education Forum (HEF), Gujarat Chapter, among others. He has developed over 150 FREE EDUCATIONAL MOBILE Apps for the Google Play Store exclusively for Teachers, Students, and Parents. This work has been recognised by the LIMCA BOOK OF RECORDS & INDIA BOOK OF RECORDS as the only Indian to draw that feast. Dr Mehrotra works as a PRINCIPAL at KUNWARS GLOBAL SCHOOL, Lucknow, in India. He has conducted over 1000 workshops globally on "Excellence In Education" integrated with Total Quality Management and Six Sigma, Technology Integration in Education (TIE), Developing towards being ROCKSTAR TEACHERS, including Cyberspace, Cyber Security, Classroom Management, School Leadership & Management, and Innovative teaching within classrooms via Mind Maps, NLP and Experiential Learning in Academics. He is an active TEDx speaker and can be viewed on the youtube TEDx channel.

As a premium UDEMY Instructor, he has developed over 450 courses and caters to over 8

Lakh students from 180 countries.

He can be visited at www.authordheerajmehrotra.com.

ABOUT THE AUTHOR

BY NATIONAL
AWARDEE
EDUCATOR
Kindle Price: ₹72.00
inclusive of all taxes
Teaching in the VUCA WORLD
Dr. Dheeraj Mehrotra
authordheerajmehrotra.com
Flipkart
available at
amazon

BY NATIONAL
AWARDEE
EDUCATOR
BASICS OF
ARTIFICIAL
INTELLIGENCE
&
MACHINE
LEARNING
DR. DHEERAJ MEHROTRA
Digital List Price: ₹103.95
Kindle Price: ₹99.00
Save ₹4.95 (4%)
inclusive of all taxes
authordheerajmehrotra.com
Flipkart
available at
amazon

101
SCHOOL
MANAGEMENT
STRATEGIES
Towards EFFECTIVE
QUALITY MANAGEMENT
System in Schools
DR. DHEERAJ
MEHROTRA
Digital List Price: ₹72.45
M.R.P.: ₹199.00
Kindle Price: ₹ 69.00
Save ₹ 130.00 (65%)
inclusive of all taxes
amazon
www.authordheerajmehrotra.com

A
PRIORITY
FOR
SCHOOLS

www.authordheerajmehrotra.com

FOR QUALITY
SCHOOLS
Towards a sustainable
future ahead
amazon
₹269.00
M.R.P.: ₹299.00
100 GREEN
SCHOOLING
IDEAS
TOWARDS A SUSTAINABLE CULTURE IN SCHOOLS
Dr. Dheeraj Mehrotra
www.authordheerajmehrotra.com

FOR
QUALITY
PARENTING
Maximizing
Learning
Potential of Kids
200
WOW PARENTING
SKILLS
DR. DHEERAJ MEHROTRA
amazon
www.authordheerajmehrotra.com
₹269.00
M.R.P.: ₹299.00